FAITH VERSUS FEAR

FAITH VERSUS FEAR

Kicking COVID-19's Butt

By

Veronica G. Tucker

ISBN: 9798582978756 (paperback)

CHAPTER 1

Life is a journey, and I intend on enjoying every moment of it! It all began on July 30, when I woke up feeling tired...just exhausted. But I pushed myself and went to work. Once at work, I was still feeling tired, but I kept working. I was so glad when the time came to go home. I came straight home and went right to bed. I was so tired.

CHAPTER 2

Friday, July 31. I woke up just as tired as I was on Thursday morning. But once again, I went on in to work. While there, a couple of times I stood up and felt dizzy, which was not normal for me. I shook it off and walked to the restroom, then returned to my seat to finish working. I made it through the day at work and I came straight home and lay down. I woke up several times during the night, with a fever this time. I thought to myself, *I wish this bronchitis would leave me alone.* Two weeks prior, I had called my doctor's office to ask about my sinus problem and bronchitis. They advised me to keep taking over-the-counter meds and told me that I would be ok. This was true, until that Thursday and Friday night two weeks later. Friday night's sleep was like no other: I had a fever during the night that was gone by morning.

CHAPTER 3

Saturday, August 1. When I woke up, I talked to God and prayed. I said, "Lord, now last night was too much to just be sinus or bronchitis because I had a fever." My mom always told me that if I have a fever in my body, then something is infected. So right then I decided that I was going to see about myself that day! Just as soon as I made that decision, my telephone rang. It was my son, Marquise.

He said, "Mama, how are you feeling today?"

I said, "I am feeling really tired and I have decided to go to urgent care today."

He said, "Ok, cool. That's a plan. I already told my wife that I was going to check on you today because you have not seen or kept the grands for two weeks now, and something has got to be going on with you!"

His wife agreed to take care of the house and babies for him to come see about me. I said, "Oh…ok."

Marquise said, "I am on the way."

I said, "Hold up. I have to clean up downstairs and get my shower. Can you give me about an hour?"

He said, "Lady, you didn't play with me. You raised me well, and I can get us breakfast and clean up downstairs for you by the time you get your shower. I got you."

I said, "Ok."

When I tell you that it took everything, I had in me to get showered and dressed…it did. I was so tired and drained. An hour later, when I went downstairs, Marquise had cleaned up and brought breakfast. He said, "Mama, I know you don't feel so good…but you look good to me."

I smiled with tears of joy in my eyes and said, "Thank you!" I had lost thirteen pounds within the last two weeks… just eating right and cutting out fried foods, sodas, and bread. So that made me feel a little bit better, but I was still tired and had shortness of breath. We ate breakfast—for me, it was four spoons of oatmeal and fruit. That was the first time I could not taste food. I was ready to go to urgent care.

CHAPTER 4

After arriving at urgent care in Fayetteville, Georgia, there was an attendant at a table outside of the building. We walked over and spoke to her and she began asking about my symptoms, which were fatigue and shortness of breath when I walk more than ten or fifteen steps. I completed the form she provided and returned to my car to wait for her to call me. About ten minutes later, she called me and asked me to go to a certain trailer that was just past her desk. Marquise and I went to the trailer and knocked on the door. A nurse opened the door and asked, "Who's sick here?"

I said, "Well he is fine, so I guess it's me."

She smiled and took my hand to help me inside. Then she turned and told Marquise that he could not come in. He said, "Oh, ok…well, when she is ready to come out, don't swing the door too wide because I will be waiting right here for my mother." She smiled and came in to examine me. She examined and took my vitals. Later, she told me that my blood pressure (which is normally high—it's the only medication I take daily, along with my natural herbs) was normal and everything was good except my oxygen. Normal oxygen levels are 94–96 percent, or they can be as high as 100 percent. My oxygen level was 91 percent. The nurse said she wanted to tell me but she did not want to scare me.

I said, "Go ahead…I am never scared. Queen Vee got King Jesus, and if something comes to me, I know He will see me through it!"

She said, "I want you to go to the emergency room."

I said, "Ok," and I stood up and thanked her for examining me. I told her that I would go straight to the ER. When the door opened, there was Marquise, standing with his hand out, saying, "Step right down, my lady."

I stepped down and began telling him about everything being good except my oxygen level. I described what a normal oxygen level is and what my oxygen was at the time. I told him that the nurse recommended that I go to the ER. He did not blink.

He said, "Ok, which hospital do you like or want to go to?"

I told him, "I really don't like to go to any of them because I have had family members die in all of them…but they are there to help people get well, and I need to go in order to get better and return home." At that point, I asked him to take me to Piedmont Fayette Hospital.

CHAPTER 5

On August 1 at about 3:30 p.m., we arrived at the ER, parked, and went to the glass sliding door out front where a nurse met us and said, "Who's sick here?"

I replied, "I am," and she said, "Ok, you can come on in, and you, sir, will have to go back."

My son responded, "Hold on. Are you telling me you are about to take my mom's hand off of my arm, take her inside, and I can't come in?"

The nurse said, "Yes," and Marquise said, "Ok, well go on and call the police because I am not leaving this parking lot until my mom comes out of here."

I said, "Wait, Marquise. What did we raise you to do?"

He said, "Think.

I said, "Ok, then. You have one minute."

Thirty seconds later he said, "Ok…Ms. Nurse, I apologize if I said anything wrong, but I am just worried about my mama!"

She said, "No need to apologize…you were fine. Like you said, you're just worried about your mom."

He said, "Ok. If I go get a cord and plug for my mom's

phone, will you get it to her so we can call, Google Duo, and text each other?"

She said, "I sure will."

With a plan in place, Marquise handed me over to the nurse and took off for the store.

CHAPTER 6

That ER room of nurses turned me every which way but loose. They tested me for everything known to man and, oh my God, that COVID test at the hospital was nothing like the one I had taken at work. They used a long Q-tip, and when they put it in my nose…I think I could feel that Q-tip dancing around in my head. It hurt so bad that I stretched my hands and legs out as far as they could go, and I tried to scream…but nothing came out! If there was COVID-19 or anything else in there, they were going to pull it out on that Q-tip.

After an EKG and all other testing, about an hour later, my nurse came back in the room and said, "You're positive."

I said, "Positive? What do you mean 'positive'? I am a fifty-four-year-old single woman, and I don't have recreational sex…so I know I am not pregnant! What are you talking about? I just took several tests today."

She said, "Positive for COVID-19."

I said, "What? Really?"

She said, "Yes."

I said, "Are you sure?"

She said, "Yes."

I said, "Well then I am ok."

She said, "Ok?"

I said, "Yes."

She said, "How is that ok?"

I said, "Well, I know God got me and I got this, and I am here to *kick some COVID-19 butt.* I love my family and life too much to give up, cave in, and quit. Let's do this…it's on. I am ready to fight! Just tell me what I need to do to get better, and I will do it, 110 percent.

She said, "Lady, I like your attitude!"

I said, "Thank you! I walk and live by faith. Now, let's get her done. COVID-19 got to go up and out of me in the name of Jesus!"

I texted my supervisor, Rodney Rooker, to advise him of my diagnosis so he could advise my co-workers, and to let him know that I would not be at work for a while. He asked if I could call him for just a minute, and I texted him back, "Yes," and called him.

He said to me, "Vee, I am so sorry this happened to you, but do me one favor."

I said, "Ok."

He said, "I want you to *kick COVID's ass*!" (in his strong, New York voice).

I said, "I am already ahead of you. I just told that nurse that I was there to *kick some COVID butt*!"

He said, "That's it! Take care and I will talk to you soon."

By this time, the other nurse walked in with a bag for me from my son. He sent me a plug, a cord, and an orange Gatorade. After receiving the package, I called him to advise him that I tested positive for COVID-19, and he said, "Oh, man."

He took a deep breath and said, "Ok, ok. Can I stay at your house?"

I said, "Sure you can."

Because he did not want to go back around his wife and the kids after being around me, he went to my house and cleaned everything I had touched, including my laptop for work and everything inside and out of the bag. My car as well as my house. He is off on weekends, so that Sunday, he did not have to work…but by Monday, he had his computers at my house, working from home and calling his mama whenever he wanted to, and I loved it. I called, used Google Duo, and FaceTime with him, my siblings, and select friends. Not everyone could handle what I was going through. I did not share it with everyone, and I even figured out that a couple of friends I shared it with were not ready for it either. But that's ok. I live by what God says, not man. I kept my distance from negative people with unfavorable things to say.

CHAPTER 7

On August 1 around 9:30 p.m., they moved me from the ER to a hospital room, where I was on level-five oxygen. They gave me shots, medication, and antibiotics and took my vitals day and night. I was still experiencing shortness of breath and just straight tired. The first nurse who came to visit and examine me was Natalie. She told me several things to help me, but the most important thing she said to me was to rotate in the bed while I sleep at night.

First, she asked me to get in the bed on my right side. I did, and then she had me turn on my back, then my left side…then my stomach. When she examined my back and my left side, there was a hard spot underneath my shoulder blade about halfway down my back. It was about the size of a pancake. She asked which side I slept on, and it was my left side. She told me that the inflammation was settling on that side because I always slept on that side and to always rotate during the night.

After we talked, she gave me a beat massage. When I tell you that that lady beat my back like an African would beat a drum, I am not lying! That lady beat my back for three minutes—hard and strong. But once she finished massaging my back, I could feel the hard spot breaking up. The massage worked, and I continued to cough up and spit out everything that came up so that I could get the inflammation out of my body. If it remained in my lungs, eventually my lungs would close up on me and I could die. That was the first time that I heard that I had pneumonia.

Nurse Natalie told me to sit on the side of the bed every morning and bend all the way over, letting my hands touch the floor, and that would stretch my lungs out daily to help keep them open. This was along with the manual breathing machine I had to use several times per hour to make my lungs stronger. She also told me to look up good gut foods, and that those are what I should eat. Whatever we put in our gut determines how we feel, from the crown of our head to the soles of our feet.

I loved talking to Natalie; she was so nice, knowledgeable, and helpful to me. I thanked her for everything she did for me and talked to me about. She not only does the job she is paid to do…but she was made to do that job, and she did it well.

When 4:00 a.m. came, like clockwork, my eyes opened and I got out of bed to start my day, as usual. I listened to my radio day and night, so I was already praising Him as I got up to pray and wash for the day. I never stayed in the bed allowing COVID to overtake my body and settle in. COVID-19 was being evicted from my body and I had to move around and spit that virus out as often as it came up.

My next nurse was Nurse Nikki. Nikki and I talked about COVID, family, and just life in general. She took my vitals, gave me a shot, and we talked for quite a while, just about how good life and God are. When we finished talking, I thanked her for all she did for me and the good conversation.

My third nurse was Nurse Woody…but for some reason I kept calling him Dr. Woody. I don't know why. I guess in my mind, a nurse should always be a woman and a man should be a doctor. But Nurse Woody was very helpful, too. He looked me over, took my vitals, and he said to me, "Ms. Tucker, I see your legs are not swollen but a little ashy, and that's fine." I looked at him sideways about that. Then he explained to me that the medicine they had me taking has been known to cause blood clots, and if I rubbed my legs or arms too hard, and if there was a blood clot in that area, it could split—go to my heart or brain and kill me. That's why they never gave me lotion or Vaseline. I said, "Oh, my."

Nurse Woody also talked to my son about COVID-19. He himself had already had COVID-19, as had two of my other nurses. He made sure he explained to us that it is possible to catch COVID-19 several times, and to be careful. "Wear your mask, wash your hands, and stay home as often as possible because we don't know where COVID is. It can be on a surface, as well as airborne."

He told my son to be very careful around his wife and kids, and Marquise told him that he had not been home since he left to come to my house on Saturday, and that day was Monday. Nurse Woody talked to Marquise a long time and advised him to get tested before he went home. I was so thankful that he took the time to talk to me and my son, giving such helpful advice and genuinely caring for me and my family. Nurse Woody was truly a helpful man during this journey.

CHAPTER 8

Each day, Dr. Bradley would stop by and talk to me. He asked me how I was doing and talked to me about my health as he checked my chart. By this time, I was feeling really good. My niece, Shanitra, had told me years ago that if you go to the hospital sick, with good insurance, your minimum stay would be three days. My sister, Rena, says that if you have the kind of insurance she does, they treat and release you like a bowling ball!

Dr. Bradley said that he and the nurses were very proud of my progress. I was always up dancing and cleaning and moving around every time they walked by my room. He said I would be going home, possibly on Tuesday or Wednesday (and that day was Monday).

I said, "No, it will be Tuesday," and smiled.

He said, "No, you don't understand."

I said, "Yes, I do, but I have had a talk with the Lord and it will be Tuesday."

He said, "Oh, ok."

He smiled and continued to check my chart. He said,

"I just love your positive attitude, and it's a joy to check on you daily. Take care and have a good day."

I said, "Thank you, and thank you all for taking such good care of me. I really appreciate it. Life is good!"

CHAPTER 9

Positive attitude. Positive vibe. Positive life. Once I was out of bed for the day, I stayed out of bed. I prayed, fixed my hair, washed, and listened to the radio every day and night as I slept. This is what I do daily anyway, so for me to listen to Praise 102.5 all day and night was normal. Most evenings I don't even turn on the television when I get home from work. While in the hospital, I listened to the radio and praised the Lord all day and night as well. When the music was of a fast beat, I stood up and did my little two-step. When the music was slow, I sat down and just meditated on the music and the word of God.

I felt better and better every day, and I used the breathing machine religiously, four and five times per hour, strengthening my lungs. By Monday morning, I could feel myself getting better. But don't get me wrong…the shots and meds were being injected day in and day out. However, I had to do, physically, what I had to do to get better, as well as keep the faith that everything was going to be all right.

CHAPTER 10

Tuesday, August 4, was finally here. When Nurse Marlene came in, I was already up fixing my hair. She said, "Good morning, Ms. Tucker. How are you today? Oh! You are fixing your hair?"

I said, "Yes. Just because I am in here, that does not mean that I don't need to look good! I am wonderful and feeling great!"

She said, "Well, good! We are so proud of your progress, and the nurses just love coming by to check on you because you have such a positive attitude and they know you are going to say something to make them laugh. Well, what can I do for you this morning?"

I said, "Can you just take this oxygen straw out of my nose? My first night here, the oxygen level was at five, and the second day they lowered it to two. But Monday, nobody said anything about that straw or this heavy heart monitor up here on my chest. I mean, it's like having a third titty on my chest and it is heavy. Please remove this heavy thing and this straw off and out of me today!"

She laughed so hard, and when she finally stood up

straight, she said, "Well, Ms. Tucker, I can take the oxygen off but not the heart monitor, and if at any time your breathing changes or bells go off, I will return to put the oxygen back on."

I said, "Ok, I got this. Here you go."

I took it out, and it felt *so good* to be free. I took it out, and she never had to put it back in. After she left and I finished getting ready for the day, I went over to the window and said to myself, "I am ready to go home. Lord, I am ready."

Moments later, the doctor came in and said that I can go home. I was released and went home by 2:30 p.m. on Tuesday, August 4. I was so elated to call my son and say, "Come on and get me. I am ready to come home!"

He said, "Cool! I am on the way!"

Marquise picked me up, masked, and we went to get my meds and some extra food. Afterward, we went to my house. I was so thankful to be home. It just felt good to be in my place of love and peace.

My son worked from home at my house for a week, just to make sure I was all right. I kept trying to send him home to his wife and children, but he would not go until he was satisfied that his mom could fully take care of herself. We wore masks around the house when we were in the same room. I took a long, warm, relaxing bath, and it felt so good! The next few days, I washed clothes, cooked my meals, took meds, and answered calls from urgent care, work, Fulton County, and my insurance company, etc. My son would check on me several times during the day, making suggestions to make things easier.

I was overloaded with telephone calls. I decided to write down dates and other information that they all wanted to know from a person who was just trying to get back to herself...if that makes any sense. They wanted to know what day I started to feel sick, where I had been, and if I had been around someone with COVID-19. The calls began when I was in the hospital, and I simply told them the truth: I don't know. I said, "You will have to call me back. I will have to think about it."

I wrote those things down as they came to mind, and I took my blood pressure and temperature every day and wrote them down, too, because the doctors called and wanted to know that. I became an "application" kind of person to help me through this, and it worked to write things down. That way I wouldn't get a headache trying to remember everything.

CHAPTER 11

Marquise went to be tested for COVID-19 and tested negative. Oh, what a great God we serve! He will get to see his kids and wife in person tonight instead of on Google Duo. It had been six days. He took his last trip to the grocery store for me and cleaned out my outside trash can. Then he was headed home to his family. I was so happy! I love and appreciate my son so much for being there for me, and his wife, Kayla, for understanding. I love them so much, and I would be remiss if I did not mention my grandkids. I love those little people to life! They make my heart smile every time I think of them: Chantz and Jordyn. That's right! I have four PJs (my pride and joy).

CHAPTER 12

Positivity and faith were the keys to my healing. While hospitalized, I had to protect my eye, ear, and heart gates. I did not watch TV at all. It has too much toxic information, and I was working on a healing. Years of teachings from my pastor taught me just what to do. I love and appreciate them so much for always being transparent with life lessons that I have been able to apply to my life and watch them manifest. They are true vessels used by the Lord to bring the Word to us. I am a proud World Changer!

I believe that there is a song for every situation and relationship in life. It's a daily thing for me to relate a song to my life and what I am going through at that time. The following are some songs I listened to every day while in the hospital that increased my faith as I went through my healing:

1. "Patiently Praising" (by Fred Jerkins, featuring Lowell Pye)
2. "It's Gonna Be Alright" (by Titus Showers, featuring Jermaine Dolly)

3. "This Week" (by Anthony Brown and group therapy)
4. "It Belongs to Me" (by Juan and Lisa Winans, featuring Marvin L. Winans)
5. "Thank You for It All" (by Marvin Sapp)
6. "I've Seen Him Work" (by Anita Wilson)
7. "Pull Us Through" (by Jermaine Dolly, featuring Maranda Curtis)

CHAPTER 13

Once I had been home for a while, I began returning calls, texting, and giving my testimony, letting them know that COVID-19 is not a joke. Stay masked up everywhere you go. Wash your hands. Put a sign on your door: "No mask, no entry!" And you can catch COVID-19 several times. I waited until twenty-plus days had passed before I went to see the older people in my life to give them my testimony and to tell them to be very careful. I could not tell them anything before I was over COVID-19 because they would have been so worried about me and I did not want that. I kept it to myself until I could see them and tell them for myself. Aunt Jean and Uncle Clifford were so grateful that I waited to tell them, and they were thankful that I am still alive. I talked to anyone who would listen. I was so excited to be alive after an experience that a lot of people did not make it through. I thank God for my life—and that's a song by Smokie Norful (I told you…there is a song for every situation and relationship in life).

When I was released from the hospital, I was so full, happy, and excited to be alive. It was like I was pregnant with a story that I had to tell. I could not sleep a full night without waking up to write down my ideas. That's when I finally realized that it was my testimony that I had to put in book form. I called my sister, Vivian, and she told me, "Your healing looks good on you, and that's your testimony."

Ok, that was confirmation that I needed to write this book. My sister, Rena, said, "I don't know what I would do without you!" I told her she would continue to live her best life. My brother, Alvin, told me, "Baby, I am just happy you beat COVID 19 and you are still alive!" I was so full that I was talking faster than I have ever talked in my life. My oldest sister told me to take a Benadryl for about three nights to slow me down. But it still took a couple of weeks for me to slow down. I had to tell this story to my forever friends and family and write the story to slow myself down.

So, this is my testimony. And I pray that it will bless someone, just reading this information, and help them if COVID-19 should come their way. Whether it tells you the signs to look out for to determine if you might have COVID-19, or ministers to your heart and increases your faith. There is another song: "Increase My faith." There are songs listed that are healing and praise songs that are nice to listen to. Information about a television fast to protect your eye, ear, and heart gates while you work on your healing.

This is my testimony. I am happy to still be alive to tell it, and I give all honor, glory, and praise to God. I love the Lord and I will forever serve and lift Him up for the rest of my life! May God bless and keep you all safe from COVID 19.